70.3

Sam Mueller

BROADWAY PLAY PUBLISHING INC
New York
www.broadwayplaypublishing.com
info@broadwayplaypublishing.com

70.3

First edition: December 2024
I S B N: 979-8-88856-045-7

Book design: Marie Donovan
Page make-up: Adobe InDesign
Typeface: Palatino

70.3 was originally commissioned and developed by The Hearth Theater (Julia Greer, Producing Artistic Director, and Emma Miller, Founding Artistic Director).

CHARACTERS & SETTING

LOLA, *this is her first triathlon. She's just lost a lot of weight.*

AVERY, *he's a decorated triathlete. He keeps himself busy.*

ROWAN, *they're (good at) running (and swimming and biking and existing).*

MARGOT, LOLA*'s ex-something. She exists mostly in* LOLA*'s stress daydreams.*

They all exist at the age where bodily ailments have to be taken seriously, where you have to start taking multivitamins, and when you start thinking there might be more you could do if you put your mind to it.

Place: Colorado
Denver, Evergreen, Idaho Springs, Golden, Boulder, around there
Storybook town
5,000-8,000 feet above sea level

NOTES

A / indicates an overlap. A guideline for when the following line will begin.

With a deep gratitude to
Parker Murphy
and
Dani Bryant

THE WARM UP

(In darkness:)

LOLA:
What do you do when you're disappearing
and people think it's you becoming?

(Then, LOLA
In a wetsuit that is worn for swimming competitions
Like the beginnings of triathlons or more specifically:
The Half Ironman that LOLA *is currently poised and ready to begin.*
More than a mile above sea level.
Badass shit)

LOLA:
I ran away.
And the running bit is supposed to come last.
It's swim, bike, run.
Every triathlon—swim. bike. run.
One of the *only* things I knew about triathlons before all of this and I still botched it.
I had to run first.
I couldn't take it anymore
Sitting surrounded by people who thought they knew me,
People who thought they could say things to me,
Who would call me things like *brave.*
I'm not brave.
Because here's the truth: I am flight over fight always.

Flight all the way, baby.
I *flew* away.
That's my Half Ironman.
Fly, swim, bike, run.
I took two trains to JFK and bought a same-day one-way ticket from an actual person behind a desk
Got on a plane
And took it all the way to Colorado.

(Then, we're there with LOLA *in Colorado.*
We're a mile up with her.
In the mountains, maybe literally, maybe not.
In any case, there is vertical space to climb, perch, and most importantly, watch.)

LOLA:
And then there I was,
staring at the front range of the *Rocky Fucking Mountains*
Thinking to myself, *holy shit, they really are huge.*
Like *of course, Lola, they're a major fucking mountain range,*
But it's just different when you're standing in front of them.
It's just different when it's real and in front of you and staring you right in the eyes.
And I couldn't help but feel small, even though I came here to not feel small
But this kind of small felt different.
And I couldn't quite say how, yet.
But at that point, it was too late.
Time to jump in.

(Water.
Possibly literally, but mostly
The sound of it, all-consuming.
We shift.)

SWIM

ONE

(A sporting good store.
LOLA *is trying to zip the wetsuit up over her swimskin.*
The sound of rushing water somewhere,
MARGOT, *up on her perch, holding a lifeguard's rescue buoy.*
Her sunglasses are on so we can't tell—is she watching?)

AVERY:
Do you need / help?

LOLA:
NO!

AVERY:
You sure? Those ones are notoriously hard / to zip up.

LOLA:
Nope, I'm fine.
I think I just need
IthinkIjustneedabiggerone.

AVERY:
No, I think that size is right.

*(*LOLA *looks at* AVERY *looking at her.)*

LOLA:
If I can't do it now, then how am I supposed to do it before a race?

AVERY:
Everyone zips each other up going to the starting line.
Even the elites
It's not a big deal

LOLA:
Yeah, but what about all the times I train with it.

AVERY:
You just attach a string to the zipper.
I'm sure there's one here with a pull attached / to it already.

LOLA:
This.
(This is exhausting for her.)
This is the one that comes in the size that I thought I would need.

AVERY:
It's supposed to fit like a glove.
Will you let me zip you up?

LOLA:
Fine.

*(*AVERY *goes to help* LOLA.*)*

AVERY:
If it makes you feel any better, the first time I competed in a wetsuit
I was so hopped up on adrenaline that I couldn't peel the wetsuit off my legs.
I literally stepped off to the side
and asked someone who was just spectating for help.
(The wetsuit zips.)
There you go.
Piece of cake.

LOLA:
Thanks.

(She goes to look at herself.)

AVERY:
I probably looked like a helpless turtle
Lying on my back on the ground

LOLA: *(Quietly)*
Oh, I think I hate this

AVERY:
So, what's it for?

LOLA:
Excuse me?

AVERY:
The suit.
What's it for.

(This is not a conversation LOLA *wants to continue having. Especially in a wetsuit.)*

LOLA:
It's like you said, actually.
Triathlons.

AVERY:
Oh!
Have we met before?

LOLA:
No, I've never been to Colorado.

AVERY:
I was going to say,
Tri community here is on the small side.
I feel like I would have remembered you.
Avery.
(He sticks his hand out.)

LOLA:
Lola.

AVERY:
Well, I look forward to maybe seeing you, Lola.
Which race?

LOLA:
Uh, the half Ironman.

AVERY:
Woah, 70.3
Okay cool.

Same.
We've got some time.

LOLA:
Kind of feels like I don't have any time at all.

AVERY:
Solid six months out.
Never done a 70.3?

LOLA:
Nope.

AVERY:
What's your longest?

LOLA:
Triathlon?

AVERY:
Yeah.

LOLA:
Nothing.

AVERY:
Nothing?
Never done a tri?

LOLA:
Never done a tri.

AVERY:
Not Olympic?

LOLA:
Not Olympic.

AVERY:
Not even a sprint?

LOLA:
Well, this is humiliating.

AVERY:
And you're signed up for the Boulder Half Iron.

LOLA:
Well, they charged my card like I am.

AVERY:
Who even are you?

LOLA:
Just…me.

AVERY:
You didn't want to start a little slower?
I'm not trying to be—

LOLA:
Impish?
Ornery?

AVERY:
Difficult.
I'm not trying to be difficult, encyclo/
Fuck, I meant thesaurus.

LOLA:
Dictionary.

AVERY:
Okay, Webster.
I'll give you a point for that.
Lola: 1
Avery: 0

LOLA:
Oh my god, did you want to make a sale today or not.

AVERY:
I don't work here.

(A moment)

LOLA:
You asked if I needed help.

AVERY:
Zipping up.

Not like,
It just looked like you were trying to zip up.

(LOLA goes to unzip herself.)

LOLA:
Okay.

AVERY:
Do you want help with that?

(LOLA gets it.)

LOLA:
Nope!!!

AVERY:
I'm just saying
Do what you've gotta do.
No shame in looking like a helpless turtle.

LOLA:
I wouldn't say *no* shame, but

AVERY:
Take my number.

LOLA:
For

AVERY:
You are *super* not from here.

LOLA:
Super not.

(AVERY waits.)

LOLA:
New York.

AVERY:
Like the state or the / city.

LOLA:
Manhattan proper.

AVERY:
As opposed to Manhattan improper.

LOLA:
Manhattan improper is not a thing.

AVERY:
We can make it a thing.

(LOLA contemplates.)

AVERY:
Take my number,
just in the case you get stranded in the middle of nature somewhere.

(LOLA takes out her phone and unlocks it.
She hands it to AVERY.)

LOLA:
Is everyone this nice here?

AVERY:
Yes.
(He puts his number in the phone.)
There's a class here on Friday nights.
There's a back room with a bunch of stationary bikes.

LOLA:
Nice.

AVERY:
You mimic the course on the bikes.
You should come take it.

LOLA:
Do you take it?

AVERY:
Sometimes, yeah.

LOLA:
Perhaps!

AVERY:
When the race gets close,
you do it together, just with breath
No music,
The way you do it in the actual race.
It helped me a lot when I was prepping for my first Ironman.
It was good to prepare for the silence.
But also, it's fun, I promise.

LOLA:
Solid maybe.

AVERY:
Welcome to Colorado, Lola.

*(*AVERY *hands her phone back.*
He climbs up to a landing of his own, apart from MARGOT*'s.*
He settles in.
We shift.)

TWO

*(*LOLA*, at the edge of a lake.*
ROWAN *is swimming.*
LOLA *is struggling with the wetsuit.*
ROWAN *swims out of the lake.*
ROWAN *doesn't notice* LOLA*, or if they do, they certainly don't care.)*

LOLA:
Ideal conditions?

ROWAN:
Um.

LOLA:
Like calm waters, but
I definitely need a wetsuit, don't I?

ROWAN:
It's cold as fuck in there.

LOLA:
Oh.
Sure.

*(*ROWAN *strips out of their wetsuit.*
They step into sweatpants and a sweatshirt that were left in a pile by the water's edge.
They take their hair out of their swim cap.)

LOLA:
Do you mind just zipping—

ROWAN:
Maybe you need a bigger size.

*(*ROWAN *grabs their things.)*

LOLA:
I thought it was supposed to fit like a glove—

*(*ROWAN *has left, climbing up to a landing.)*

LOLA:
Cool cool cool.
(She struggles.
It's kind of painful to watch, a slice of awkward intimacy.
But she fucking does it.
Then she looks at the lake.)
Well. Don't drown, Lola.
(She wades in.)

THREE

*(*LOLA *swims.*
MARGOT *lifts her sunglasses from her face.*
She speaks from the landing.)

MARGOT:
You know, a text would have been nice.

*(*LOLA *keeps swimming, trying to ignore* MARGOT.*)*

LOLA:
Not now. Not now. Not now…

MARGOT:
A phone call seems like it would have been a stretch.

LOLA:
How do I get you out of here?

MARGOT:
I don't know, love.
It's your brain, not mine.

LOLA:
I don't want to hear it.

MARGOT:
Seems like you do want to hear it.
You're the one that's played my voicemail one million times.

LOLA:
I am trying to swim here.

MARGOT:
Do you have it memorized yet?
Let's see—

LOLA:
No!

*(*MARGOT *raises a megaphone to her mouth.)*

MARGOT:
(In voicemail): Lola! Hi. Look, I'm standing in your apartment right now. Don't be mad. I was worried you were dead. I don't think you're dead, but your duffle bag is gone. Where are you?

LOLA:
You don't need to know!
(She goes back to swimming.)

MARGOT:
(In voicemail) Your iPhone says you're in Colorado right now, which seems wrong, because you literally know no one who lives outside of New York City.

LOLA:
That's not true.
I know people.
Maybe not anyone in Colorado,
But I know people!

MARGOT:
(In voicemail) So I don't know if you mailed your iPhone somewhere because you're being that avoidant or for some batshit reason, you got on a plane.

LOLA:
How do you know where I am!

*(*MARGOT *lowers the megaphone.)*

MARGOT:
Don't you remember? We shared locations that night we got too drunk at / Cubby.

LOLA:
Fuck, Cubby.

MARGOT:
I walked you to 14th street and you smelled like Santal and it was really cold for May and we were both so / underdressed—

LOLA:
Yes! Okay! I remember!

MARGOT:
And we had stopped at Donut Pub which is an A+ choice for midnight Chelsea snacking and you got a s'mores cronut. I can't remember what I got…

LOLA:
Captain crunch donut.

(Into the megaphone)

MARGOT:
(In voicemail) Anyways, I don't know what's been going on with you lately but I hope this isn't one of those ideas you have where for a week you commit to it one hundred percent and then it just. Well.

LOLA:
Ouch.

MARGOT:
(In voicemail) I just hope you haven't lost your grip on reality.

LOLA:
Yeah, honestly, me too.

MARGOT:
(In voicemail) I watered your plants for you.

LOLA:
That is so / Margot of you, Margot.

MARGOT:
(In voicemail) And I know that is so Margot of me, but at least one of us is acting like ourselves.
Come on Lola.
Call me back.

*(*LOLA *swims.*
We shift.)

FOUR

(While swimming:)

LOLA:
I wanted that feeling,
the feeling of being submerged
I wanted to give my body over, feel smooth at the edges.

I wanted to be able to spend time with myself.
In my own head.
Alone.
I hoped
The noise would drop out.
Or if the noise didn't drop out,
I could make friends with it.
It could be the two of us:
The noise and me,
Held in the buoyancy.
Slowly becoming rhythmic.
But it isn't like that when it happens.

(The water, louder, wilder)

LOLA:
Limbs flailing everywhere—
kicks from other bodies knock the air from my lungs.
We are a school of fish, an invisible shark behind us,
The rushing of blood in my ears like a twisted metronome.
When I'm not worrying about drowning,
I'm worrying about not finishing fast enough and being cut from the race,
The swim stretches out before me for what seems like a never-ending baptism,
But then I feel the beach under my feet again.
(She gets out of the water.
We are in the transition between swim and bike.
The wetsuit and swim cap come off.
She slips her feet into cycling shoes.)
I'm vaguely aware people are cheering.
Music is bumping for the sake of the spectators
But one-point-two miles in the water have changed me,
Built a new world for me to live in.
As I clip into my pedal,
I hope that world can be good to me.

(We shift.)

BIKE

FIVE

*(*LOLA *is setting up and clipping in to the bike.*
MARGOT *is overly excited, coming down from her landing.*
Gone is the lifeguard buoy.
In its place is a green juice.
She's pulled on cycling shorts and a tank top.)

MARGOT:
So, you'll come here
But all those times I asked you to come down to
Tribeca and / take class

LOLA:
Okay, this isn't some candlelit
Bike to the music
People dancing in the aisles
Do weird movements on the bike—

MARGOT:
Choreography

LOLA:
Whatever
It's not that.

MARGOT:
I told you so many times.
It's not what you think.
It's not like I asked you to join a cult.

LOLA:
It's a little cultish.

MARGOT:
You never even tried it!

LOLA:
The vibes were culty.
That was enough.

MARGOT:
I'm pissed.

LOLA:
Because I wouldn't go to spin class with you and forty middle-aged white women who have enough money to buy a loft in Tribeca?

MARGOT:
Yes.
And also you're looking for Avery.

LOLA:
I'm not looking for him.

MARGOT:
Well, good, because he's not here.

LOLA:
I am *literally* just making sure no one is coming over to talk to me.
People do that here, remember?

(ROWAN *comes down from their landing.*
They take the bike that is set up at the front.
They're leading class.)

MARGOT:
I'm unconvinced.

LOLA:
If I really wanted him here,
I would have texted him and asked him to come.
I don't want anyone here.
I don't want *you* here.

*(*MARGOT *is stung.*
ROWAN *puts a headset on.)*

ROWAN:
Too late to unclip now.

LOLA:
Fuck me.

*(*ROWAN *presses play on the music.*
It is not entirely unlike the music you would hear at a cult-adjacent indoor cycling class.)

ROWAN:
Roll your wrists out.
Draw your belly button / back to your spine.

MARGOT: *(Whispered)*
Back to your spine!
Oh,
Lola,
Welcome to the cult.

ROWAN:
Don't forget to breathe.

LOLA: *(Whispered)*
Do you think they are going to recognize me?

ROWAN:
Roll your shoulders back and down.
(They bike.)

MARGOT:
(Whispered) Oh my god, remember what I told you?
(She lifts the megaphone to her mouth.)
One day, you're gonna go to class
And you're gonna want to join the endorphin cult.
I know you,
You're gonna love it

LOLA:
I still have time to hate it.

*(*ROWAN *abruptly turns the music down.)*

ROWAN:
And for anyone who hasn't been here before
If you're going to spend the whole time talking under your breath
You can either get your head in the game
Or get the fuck out.

(A moment.
LOLA *makes the choice to stay.*
ROWAN *turns the music back up.*
And then, like nothing has happened.
MARGOT *climbs back up to her perch.*
The music starts to fade out.
The class fades away.
ROWAN *climbs back up to a landing.*
We're left with pedaling and breathing.
The pedal strokes get harder.
A small pop.
LOLA *looks at her front tire.*
She comes to a stop,
Foot unclipped, breathing heavy.)

LOLA:
Oh, fuck.

(The bike has a flat.
LOLA *looks up to* MARGOT.
Then, over to AVERY.
He comes down to join her.)

SIX

AVERY:
There she is!
Avery: 2
Lola: 0

LOLA:
I've earned points when you haven't been around!
Avery: 2
Lola: At least 7
Maybe minus 1 because of this flat.

AVERY:
It's okay, everyone gets a flat tire.

LOLA:
I didn't have anyone else to text.

AVERY:
Yeah, I know, it's been like a week since I gave you my number.
You clearly didn't want to reach out.
If you hadn't popped a flat at the / top of a monster hill—

LOLA:
Oh my god, that's not it. You said that number was for / emergencies.

AVERY:
Calm down, Manhattan Proper. I'm joking.

LOLA:
I know.

(Reader: she did not know.)

AVERY:
You can use it just to say hi, though.

(He grabs a hold of the handlebars on the bike and starts to downshift the gears.)

LOLA:
You gave me your number for emergencies and then an emergency happened.
You jinxed it.

AVERY:
And now I'll fix it.
(He takes a few things out of his backpack and tosses them on the ground.
He starts to release the wheel from the bike.
Releasing the level, loosening a screw, making sure there's slack in the chain.)

LOLA:
You were wrong, by the way.

AVERY:
An odd thing to say to someone fixing your flat for you.

LOLA:
You said everyone here was nice.

AVERY:
Did someone hurt your feelings?

LOLA:
Um, yes, and then they turned out to be the instructor teaching that class you told me about.

AVERY:
You went to class?
Wow, I really didn't think you would.

LOLA:
Yeah, I went to class.
That's gotta count for a point.

AVERY:
Fine.
(He lifts the bike up by the handlebars and bounces it to get the wheel to pop loose.
There is, of course, a more elegant way to do this but Avery is strong enough, so that's that.
He unscrews the air valve and lets the rest of the air out of the tire.)
Avery: 2
Lola: 1

LOLA:
Avery: 1
Lola: 1
You get a point taken away because not everyone is nice.

AVERY:
Sure, fine, Rowan's a bit sharp with new people.
We're even.

(He thinks a moment.)
Come hold this.

*(*LOLA *holds the lip of the bike tire and he uses a bike lever until the tire is half on and half off the wheel.*
AVERY *slides the tube out.*
He studies it over the following:)

AVERY:
But you've gotta admit,
the way they craft class is like a fucking *art* form

LOLA:
Well, your crush was rude as fuck to me.

AVERY:
Not a crush. Why are you so concerned with my relationship to Rowan?

LOLA:
I'm just trying to figure out why you love them so much.

AVERY:
They coached me through my first full Ironman.

LOLA:
Fine.

AVERY:
I *will* be honest.
They were also my prom date.

*(*LOLA *laughs.)*

LOLA:
I *knew* it.

AVERY:
No, I don't want to get caught in a technicality here so I was honest.
I will not lose points on a technicality.
We went to prom as friends and it was a decade ago.

LOLA:
Small towns kill me.

AVERY:
Will you check the tire?

(LOLA checks the outside of the tire while AVERY pulls out a new bike tube.)

LOLA:
It seems fine.

AVERY:
The inside too?

(AVERY takes the wheel from LOLA.)

AVERY:
Usually if you slip your fingers in
...
and slide them slowly
...
You can find
...
*(He finds a rock.
He pulls it out.)*
The culprit.

*(AVERY hands it to LOLA.
He puts the new tube to his mouth.)*

LOLA:
Well, I don't think they like me.
Rowan.

AVERY:
Nah, they just see you letting your bullshit win.

*(LOLA shoots AVERY a look.
He starts to fit the tube back into the tire.)*

AVERY:
Everyone's got some.
It all rises to the surface when you're training for

something like this.
...
You want to hold the bike up for me?

LOLA:
Sure.
(She holds the bike up by the handlebars.
AVERY *puts the wheel back in.*
The exact reverse of taking it off.
He takes a can of compressed air and fills the tire up more.)

LOLA:
Thank you.

AVERY:
You are welcome.

*(*LOLA *checks out the bike.)*

AVERY:
God, but what a place to stop.

LOLA:
It's a good overlook.

*(*AVERY *wanders over to the edge.)*

AVERY:
Come see.

LOLA:
Um, I'd rather not.

AVERY:
Scared?

LOLA:
You're a person who is hot in theory and in practice.

AVERY:
I meant scared of heights.
It's a steep drop.

LOLA:
I was in the middle of a ride.
I should get back—

AVERY:
The miles will always be there, Lola.

(LOLA hesitates.
She puts the bike down gently and walks over.)

LOLA:
Wow.
Jesus.

AVERY:
He had nothing to do with this.
This is all Mama Nature.

LOLA:
That was extremely mountain man of you.

(LOLA and AVERY look out.)

AVERY:
It's a nice bike by the way.

LOLA:
Thank you.
I'm still getting used to it.

AVERY:
Is the new seat kicking your ass?

LOLA:
It's mostly the pedals.
Yesterday, I fell over trying to unclip from them and that is embarrassing in both theory and in practice.
I thought I was going to twist my ankle getting my shoe out.

AVERY:
Did you try some lube on the pedals?
I have some WD-40.
Your clips will slip right in and out.

LOLA:
Sure.

AVERY:
I'll bring it.
Next time.
When we go for a ride together.

*(*AVERY *wipes a greasy hand on his pants.*
He holds it out for LOLA *to shake.)*

LOLA:
. . .
You win, Mountain Man.

AVERY:
I always do, Manhattan Proper.

*(*LOLA *and* AVERY *shake on it.*
He leaves her, looking out at the Rockies.
He climbs back up to his landing.
After a moment, she looks back to the bike.
She goes back to it.
She clips her feet in.
She pedals and pedals.
Music begins to fade back in.
We shift.)

SEVEN

(The cycling room.
It's just LOLA*, pedaling.*
MARGOT *is holding a copy of* Bicycling *magazine.*
ROWAN *descends, holding the things they will need to teach class.*
A moment)

ROWAN:
You're early.

*(*LOLA *slows, but she doesn't stop.*
She will not stop pedaling this whole time.)

LOLA:
I was actually hoping to catch you.

ROWAN:
I didn't think you would come back,
the way you disappeared during the stretch last week.

LOLA:
I want to hire you.

(A moment)

ROWAN:
I don't do personal coaching anymore.
You want my instruction,
You can stay for / Friday night class.

LOLA:
I will pay you twice what you used to ask.

ROWAN:
I won't take it.

LOLA:
I will pay you what a pro athlete would pay you for something like this.

ROWAN:
No, you won't.

LOLA:
You're right.
I won't.
I don't know how much that costs but I know I don't have it.
I can take out a personal loan if I can't pay you what you're worth.

ROWAN:
That would be extremely stupid.

LOLA:
And ultimately none of your business.

ROWAN:
Why?

LOLA:
Doesn't matter.

ROWAN:
No, it's the only thing that matters.
I can't force you through training.
I can't do the race for you.
If you're gonna bail on me in the middle of this then it's not worth doing.

LOLA:
I've got a lot of bullshit.

(ROWAN *starts to set up their bike for class.)*

ROWAN:
Same.
Bullshit doesn't make you special.

LOLA:
I heard you were good at cutting through the bullshit.

(ROWAN *laughs.)*

ROWAN:
You spoke to Avery.
God, he loves to talk.

LOLA:
I have no one out here.

ROWAN:
Sounds like you've got Avery.

LOLA:
I'm out here all alone
and I still can't get other people's bullshit out of my head.

*(*ROWAN *tests the music for class.*
It should hit hard and stay jarring.
They play with the music level.
LOLA *is patient.)*

LOLA:
Why don't you want to coach anymore?

ROWAN:
It's like you said.
Bullshit.
My own bullshit.
If you can be vague about it, so can I.
Now,
Are you sticking around for class?

LOLA:
I lost a shit ton of weight.

*(*ROWAN *stops setting things up.*
MARGOT *looks up.*
They look at LOLA *and wait for her to go on.)*

LOLA:
Thank you for not saying congratulations or some fucked up shit like that.

*(*ROWAN *shrugs.)*

ROWAN:
I don't know your life.

LOLA:
I lost a shit ton of weight.
I didn't mean to, not at first at least,
and for months it was
Taking up so much space.
Like, people at the office would think for some reason that I wanted to talk about my body at any given moment.
And when it started, people didn't even know why they were saying anything at all,

they would just say
Wow, you look so good or
What did you do differently
And I would straight up lie and be like
Oh I just lightened my hair a little or
I got new conditioner
And then I lost more and it became obvious what had changed
And the comments got more and more pointed and sometimes just plain blunt
at which point it started to also be comments on photos on the internet
and DMs from people I went to high school with
whom I had not talked to in years who started saying
Oh my god, I'm so proud of you.
And then it was my friends.
Loudly, sometimes.
In public.
And I liked it.
For a while I liked it,
I ate it up.
I started to do really stupid shit to make sure it would keep happening,
But then it started to taste sour.
And people really thought they were doing a good thing but I walked into a restaurant for lunch with my friends and one of them just said,
Damn, Lola, you look so good!!!
And I snapped.
It felt like my spinal cord snapped,
Underneath the idea that my body was better, or prettier, or worthier now
and under the pressure to do whatever it takes to maintain this or even get smaller.
And I had this voice in my head I had never heard before
Whispering

Everyone's looking at you now.
Are you small enough for everyone yet?
And I never sat down for lunch.
I literally turned around and left the restaurant and had an awful conversation with my ex-girlfriend because she tried to run after me to see what was wrong
But things had been wrong for a long time.
And the only thing I had when shit got really wrong was knowing that when I do something *with* my body,
I stop thinking *about* my body.
And I've always been a cyclist,
and swimming makes me feel so free,
and running is something I always assumed I wasn't built for until I realized I could.

ROWAN:
And Boulder, because…

LOLA:
No one knows who the fuck I am here.
And I don't really know you, but I know you won't let me give up on myself.
And I'm worried I might.
And all of this can't be for nothing.

(A very long pause)

ROWAN:
How long have you been moving your legs?

LOLA:
About an hour.

ROWAN:
Alright.
If your head is telling you to stop
Or to slow down right now,
That's right where I want you
In that hard spot where you can't imagine continuing because you think the tank is empty.

Tell your head to wait.
Tell your legs to speed up.
(They stand right in front of the handlebars.)
Run me over!
Let's go!

*(*LOLA *pedals.*
And pedals.
ROWAN *ascends back to their landing.*
We shift.)

EIGHT

*(*LOLA *bikes.*
She is outside.
MARGOT *stands to survey the scenery.)*

MARGOT:
God, it's stunning out today.

*(*LOLA *ignores* MARGOT.*)*

MARGOT:
Wind through your hair.
Well.
If you can feel any wind through that helmet.

(Ignored again)

MARGOT:
The best part of being in your head is that I don't get to wear a helmet like a badass.

LOLA:
It's not badass, it's stupid.

MARGOT:
Ha! Got you!
I knew I'd get you with a helmet quip.

LOLA:
I like my brains inside my skull,

And you outside of my head.
Get OUT.

(Into the megaphone.)

MARGOT:
(Voicemail): Lola, you turned off your location settings.

LOLA:
I should have already turned them off.

MARGOT:
(Voicemail): I know you're still in Colorado. I can feel it.

LOLA:
That's fine but at least this way you don't get my real-time tracking.

MARGOT:
(Voicemail:) If you would call me back, I wouldn't have to check on you.

LOLA:
I don't want to talk to you, I think that's super clear.

*(*MARGOT *puts the megaphone down.)*

MARGOT:
And yet, here I am.

LOLA:
Don't get too comfy.

MARGOT:
Are you going to sleep with your coach?

LOLA:
Oh my *actual* god.

MARGOT:
Big hot-for-teacher vibes.

LOLA:
NO.

MARGOT:
Are you gonna sleep with that annoying guy.

LOLA:
He's not annoying.

MARGOT:
You know,
I know you had a flat kit and you called him anyways.

LOLA:
Fine.
I had a flat kit.
But I've never used one myself.
I would always just take mine to the shop and have them fix it.
I could have figured it out but I didn't want to, okay?

MARGOT:
So you are going to sleep with him.

LOLA:
I'm not sleeping with *anyone!*
I'm just trying to not *die* while I do this.

*(*MARGOT *flips the page of the magazine.)*

MARGOT:
Okay.

*(*LOLA *bikes.*
MARGOT *flips.)*

MARGOT:
You called him hot in theory and in practice.
And he heard you.

LOLA:
I'm sure I'm not the first person to call him hot.

MARGOT:
Whatever makes you feel less embarrassed.

LOLA:
It's not a *thing.*
Don't make it a thing.

MARGOT:
You watched him change that tire and you thought—

LOLA:
And I thought
Wow, I am so out of practice with this.
That is what I thought.
Are you happy now?

MARGOT:
I'm obviously not happy that you're thinking of someone else.

LOLA:
It's like that part of my brain shut off, okay.
Light switch flip.
I see people I'm attracted to
And I recognize that attraction
And that's it.
I don't know how to go from that initial attraction
To
Anywhere close to wanting, I guess.

MARGOT:
Lola, you don't have to start over.
I want you still.
I'm calling and texting and I even emailed your work email the other day.
And you must want me back, because here I am.

LOLA:
I don't even know how to want myself.
I don't know who I am when I look in a mirror anymore
And everything I see in the mirror keeps changing
Like hourly
Every time I turn and check
It's like a funhouse mirror
So how am I supposed to have a body
Even remotely near another person right now.

Like if I try to think about putting my mouth on his mouth
I—
(She checks her watch.)
Look, I need to get into this later.
I have to keep my heart rate in the one-thirties on this ride
Or Rowan's gonna be really disappointed.

MARGOT:
I'm going to keep calling.

*(*MARGOT *sits and opens her magazine.*
LOLA *rides.*
Music fades in.
We shift.)

NINE

(We are indoors.
ROWAN *descends from their landing.)*

ROWAN:
You left the room for a second.

LOLA:
What?

ROWAN:
I mean, you were pedaling
But the music stopped and I asked you / if you wanted

LOLA:
Oh

ROWAN:
Me to put more music on for you.
Where'd you go in there?

LOLA:
Just rote movement, I guess.

ROWAN:
It looked like you were having an out of body experience.

LOLA:
It's fine.

ROWAN:
It's not fine.
Your form was trash.

LOLA:
Sorry, I'm just tired.
I did so many meters in the lake this morning.

ROWAN:
So you get to half-ass the bike?

LOLA:
I didn't say that.

ROWAN:
I just want your head in the game.

LOLA:
It's here.

ROWAN:
Not at the rate you've been declining all those phone calls that keep coming in.

LOLA:
Scam calls.

ROWAN:
You've saved your scam callers by their first names?
(A point to them)
I don't care who keeps calling,
Just don't lie.

LOLA:
Fine.

ROWAN:
Are you staying for class?

LOLA:
Yes.

ROWAN:
Are you going to slump like that in class.

LOLA:
Maybe.

(ROWAN glares.)

ROWAN:
If you're going to slump, you can go home.

LOLA:
Yeah, right.

ROWAN:
I mean it.
If you're going to slump then just take the night.
Don't fuck up your back.

LOLA:
I won't slump

ROWAN:
And move up to the front.

LOLA:
But this is my spot.

ROWAN:
Not anymore.

LOLA:
Is it compulsory that I move up to the front?

ROWAN:
Don't whip out your big words as a distraction.

LOLA:
Mandatory.

ROWAN:
No, it is not *obligatory* that you move up.
See, I've got big words too.

LOLA:
Okay.

ROWAN:
You can keep hiding if you want to.
(More points to them)

LOLA:
I just prefer being in the middle.

ROWAN:
The back

LOLA:
It's the middle.

ROWAN:
When this place is full, sure.
Friday night?
Not peak class time.
You're an island back there.

LOLA:
Am not.

ROWAN:
Are too.

LOLA:
Am NOT.

ROWAN:
You should not be scared of the front row.

LOLA:
So now you want me all the way in the front row?!

ROWAN:
Your comfort zone is going to be your downfall.
Think of it as a gentle nudge.

LOLA:
Next week.

ROWAN:
You could have trained for this anywhere, dude.
You could have picked anywhere.
Popped an altitude mask on and trained from
Santa Monica, or
Raleigh
But you didn't
You flew here
And it's different energy when you're in the pack of people.

LOLA:
It's not like a different zip code back here.

ROWAN:
It's different in the middle of it.

LOLA:
I promise.

ROWAN:
Okay, the thing is, I know you're going to like it
So just do it.
I'll move your shit for you.

(ROWAN takes LOLA's water bottle from her bike.)

LOLA:
So I don't have a choice after all.

ROWAN:
You've zipped yourself into this tiny cocoon.

LOLA:
Is that not where larvae become butterflies?

ROWAN:
You're at risk of being that one that never pushes its way through.

LOLA:
Rude.

ROWAN:
I don't advise that everyone move up.
This isn't some tactic I use with everyone.
I think you can thrive up here
And I think you're drowning back there.

LOLA:
This is a bike, not a pool.

ROWAN:
If you can tell me honestly why you want to stay back there
Then maybe you can stay back there.

LOLA:
I don't want people looking at me.

ROWAN:
We turn the lights off for class.
Next!

LOLA:
We turn most of the lights off, but if I sit in the front, people will see me.

ROWAN:
Because I am a glowing ball of sunshine radiating light on everything I see?

LOLA:
I will be
Silhouetted

ROWAN:
And being a silhouette to someone scares you?

LOLA:
It distracts me.

ROWAN:
Okay, but you're very good at this.
Usually your form is great and you work hard.
Next!

LOLA:
Stop making me justify this
I don't like hearing it out loud.

ROWAN:
People have eyes.
You can't control people looking at you.

LOLA:
No, but I can
Minimize the occurrence.

ROWAN:
People are going to look at you while you do this race
And you're going to be so grateful for them while they do it
You're going to hate the parts where there's no one around.
That's a given.

LOLA:
Give me my water back.

ROWAN:
The work we do in here doesn't have to be pretty.
And in fact, the uglier it gets the better the work is, usually.
I'm not asking you for pretty,
I'm asking you to come up to the front and be real.

LOLA:
Fine.

ROWAN:
I'm asking you to come up to the front and be shamelessly good at this.

LOLA:
Let's not go that far.

ROWAN:
Show off.
Try to show off.

I'm giving you permission.
Peacock.

LOLA:
I can't do that.

ROWAN:
Oh, god, you think because you don't know how to peacock out there,
You can't peacock in here.

LOLA:
Not at all.

ROWAN:
Oh this is a huge oversight—

LOLA:
To hit the right angle
Or like
And figure out the lighting
And find the balance of candid and—

ROWAN:
Well, none of it is candid.
We can start there.

LOLA:
But it's got this candid feel.

ROWAN:
No it doesn't.
You're confusing candid with confident.
No one is candidly caught with their hips quarter angled
It's peacocking, Lola.
It's shamelessly showing off.

LOLA:
And you just,
Do it.

ROWAN:
Yeah.
You do.
If you want.
If you want external validation.
And external validation gets a bad rap but
We are pack animals.

LOLA:
And people just learned this?

ROWAN:
I don't think peacocking is a precise art.
And peacocking in here is different
On purpose.
No smoke and mirrors.
It's my world in here and in my world, I want real.

LOLA:
Real.

ROWAN:
Sweat dripping
Lungs working
Heart pumping
Real.

*(*ROWAN *tests the music for class.*
LOLA *pedals.)*

TEN

*(*LOLA *and* AVERY *on bikes.*
Flat road)

AVERY:
Has Rowan given you the fellow traveler speech yet?

LOLA:
You should be asking how many times I've heard the speech.

That person in front of you?
Not your competition.
That person is your teammate.

LOLA:
Your fellow traveler.

AVERY:
Your fellow traveler.
You don't know their body,
their injuries, their history.

LOLA:
And they don't know yours.

AVERY:
So all that should be there is mutual respect.

LOLA:
Yeah, it's a good speech.
And it's true, right,
We're all doing the same course at the same time but
It's more like running a million individual races alongside each other.

AVERY:
Although sometimes during a race,
when I get bored,
I do try to pass the person in front of me for the sport of it.
Don't tell Rowan.

LOLA:
I wouldn't throw you under the bus like that.
Although I'm sure they have great embarrassing collateral against you,
So maybe I would.

AVERY:
That's not fair, no one has embarrassing collateral against you here.

LOLA:
Oh I know, it's really nice.

AVERY:
You know, I don't think I could do what you did.
Up and leave my life.

LOLA:
You're probably too scared to make the changes you want.

AVERY:
I left for school.
I did the really big city thing.

LOLA:
Were you a New Yorker for a while?

AVERY:
Chicago.

LOLA:
Kind of / counts.

AVERY:
Shut up.
That place is huge.

LOLA:
I feel like if everyone has a back porch, it's different.

AVERY:
If New York had a great fire,
They'd have alleys and back porches too, okay?
Chicago just had a chance to start over smarter.
Okay, Manhattan Proper?
Maybe you know a little something about starting over?

LOLA:
Fine.
One point to you for a solid point made.

AVERY:
I loved that place.
I loved hearing the elevated trains.

I loved reading at the lake.
I loved all of that Midwestern food.
Dripping in butter
Deep fry it all
Serve it on a stick
It's the only place in the whole world where I want a sandwich to be wet.

LOLA:
So why'd you leave?

AVERY:
It wasn't wild enough.

LOLA:
Like actual wilderness?

AVERY:
Yes, actual wilderness but something else, too.
When I was trying to figure out if I was going to stay in Chicago or come back home,
I treated myself to a really nice hotel room with a View of Lake Michigan
And it stormed the whole weekend.
I remember looking out of the window
With a room service cocktail in my hands
And the swells in the lake were so big they were crashing onto Lake Shore Drive
Just tons of water flooding the road
Cars driving slowly, drivers probably terrified that they would get swept away
And I kept thinking
I want to be around that power all the time.
I want to immerse myself in it.
I want to feel
Small and at the same time a part of something giant.
You sit up here and you look at all this and
You feel electricity in your blood.

(He looks over at her.)
You look terrified.

LOLA:
I feel like it might make me unravel at the seams a little bit.

AVERY:
You say that like it's a bad thing.

LOLA:
I am trying quite hard to keep it all together.
…
What.

AVERY:
Nothing.

LOLA:
No.
What.
You think I'm a fucking mess?

AVERY:
I just think it's more fun to fall apart
And trust this place can catch all the pieces.

(LOLA considers.)

LOLA:
I just can't trust it yet.
I love New York,
I feel New York in my bone marrow.
Everything here is just really new?
Not just my surroundings
I feel really new in a lot of ways.

AVERY:
What changed?

(A decision is made.)

LOLA:
I bought a bike.

AVERY:
Bikes are a gateway drug.

LOLA:
I bought it to commute
But then I was using it just for fun
And then I was waking up early on Saturday mornings to cross the George Washington Bridge.
And I bought a pair of running shoes.
And I liked it, I liked being self-sufficient like that.
I liked seeing the city like that
Moving through it, seeing it as a living thing without disappearing underground to get from place to place.

AVERY:
There it is.

LOLA:
I got a promotion and I could afford all the things that kept popping up—
Physical therapy for strained ankle, strength training.
I started working from home so I had more freedom.
The routine changed.
I changed.
The people around me didn't.
I don't think they'd been seeing me
Nonetheless supporting me
For a long time.

AVERY:
And rather than find new people you just said
Fuck people altogether?

LOLA:
All I want is a bike.

AVERY:
And maybe a person to change your flat tire for you.

LOLA:
Wow, you're gonna milk that for all it's worth, huh?

AVERY:
That's the catch about all this nature, Lola.
You can't make it alone.
It will always win.

(We shift.)

ELEVEN

*(*LOLA, *finishing an indoor session with* ROWAN. MARGOT *is there, reading her magazine.)*

ROWAN:
Good.

LOLA:
Yes?

ROWAN:
Yeah, I mean,
the work is good, Lola.

LOLA:
Good.

ROWAN:
And the next two days you train outside.

LOLA:
Yes.
Hills.

ROWAN:
And then you take Thursday off.

LOLA:
Rest.

ROWAN:
And then I'll see you in class.

LOLA:
Yep.

ROWAN:
And you're not feeling like you have to throw up?

LOLA:
Nope.

ROWAN:
So the fuel plan is a go

LOLA:
And it's finally warm enough to swim in the lake
without a wetsuit.

*(*ROWAN *holds up their hand.*
LOLA *high fives it.*
MARGOT *looks over at the noise and then back to her magazine.)*

ROWAN:
Wanted to talk to you about something.

LOLA:
Oooooh,
Sounds bad
Not gonna lie

ROWAN:
You are stuck on this bicycle for
(They check their watch.)
Thirty more minutes.

LOLA:
So you've trapped me.

ROWAN:
I know you love all that dopamine from making a great escape.
But you can't run away from me right now.

LOLA:
Is this a push to make me part of a community again?

ROWAN:
Was I wrong, though?
Who rides front row every Friday?

LOLA:
Me.

ROWAN:
I love being right.
I love it so much.

LOLA:
Is this an official part of my training plan

ROWAN:
Okay, go with me here.
I'm concerned that you're about to get stuck.

LOLA:
How can you tell?

ROWAN:
It just feels like there's something taking up space in the room with us
And I don't want it to start derailing all your work.

*(*MARGOT *closes the magazine.*
She's paying attention now.)

LOLA:
Nope, just me here.

ROWAN:
No, it's like all over.

LOLA:
Are you a psychic now?

ROWAN:
Did I touch a nerve?

LOLA:
Are you trying to provoke me?
Stop it.

ROWAN:
Do you think I enjoy talking about auras?
Something is stagnant and it needs to be moving.
I'm just saying if you want to be mad, get big mad.
I can take it.

LOLA:
I don't want to be mad.

ROWAN:
Because it's uncomfortable to be mad?

LOLA:
Because I'm not mad.

ROWAN:
Are you sure?
You want to be
…something.
It's just getting stuck.

LOLA:
It's my personal life

ROWAN:
Okay, fine
Do you have a plan?

LOLA:
Uh, work around it.

ROWAN:
Ah, I see, here's the issue
Just SAY IT
Just LET YOURSELF
You gotta go THROUGH IT

*(*MARGOT *stands.*
LOLA *gets mad.)*

LOLA:
I used to not give a fuck.
Can you believe that?

ROWAN:
I can.

LOLA:
I used to let people in.
And all they did was fuck it up.
The more I got to know them, the worse they got.

ROWAN:
Some people suck.

LOLA:
But you all are right, okay?
You're right.
Lola: 0, Rowan and Avery: Ten Thousand.
You need people out here.
Are you happy now?
You win.
You have an insurmountable lead over me.

ROWAN:
It's not about me being first.
It's about you letting things flow through you so that you don't get stuck thirty-five miles into something with just as much left to go

LOLA:
Would you have been this nice to me before?

ROWAN:
There it is.
I knew I was / right.
There is something.

LOLA:
I get it.
You like being right.

ROWAN:
I would have treated you the exact same.

LOLA:
Not everyone is like that.

ROWAN:
Okay, well I'm a brand new person in your life.

LOLA:
How can you tell the difference
Between the people who belong in your life and the people who don't?

ROWAN:
Who is invested in your growth.
Who asks about it.
Who stays curious.

LOLA:
Mmm.

ROWAN:
Or you trust your gut.

LOLA:
My gut's fucked.

ROWAN:
Be kind to yourself.

LOLA:
I appreciate that, actually.

ROWAN:
See?
Not all conflict needs to be hard.

LOLA:
And not all our shit needs to match for you to get it?
Like your life doesn't need to echo mine.
I'm not wrong for asking you to give me
Empathy.
Fuck.

ROWAN:
You're moving mountains inside your mind right now, aren't you?

LOLA:
The mountains don't move, dude.
They just stand there and loom.

ROWAN:
No one ever said being with people was easy.
We just said you need people.

LOLA:
And what if I let people in
And they turn out to be horrible, shallow people

(MARGOT *sits and hides behind the magazine.)*

ROWAN:
Well, then we aren't talking about me anymore.

LOLA:
Like what if I make a mistake and let someone in who doesn't belong there?

ROWAN:
Then you take them out.

LOLA:
Has there ever been a part of Avery's / life

ROWAN:
Nooooooooo Nope
Nope
I don't want names.
I'm staying out of it.
At the finish line, you can ask me anything you want.
I'll even pull up photos of seventh grade because no one
NO ONE
Makes it out of middle school without an awkward phase
But not a second before the finish line.
Because right now, I'm your coach.
And then, I just might be your friend.

LOLA:
Might be?

ROWAN:
Stop fishing for secure connection.
Just trust it.

LOLA:
Ugh.

ROWAN:
Gross, right?
Trust?

LOLA:
The worst.

ROWAN:
I'll see you Friday.

(We shift.)

TWELVE

*(*LOLA *bikes.*
Loud music.
Nasty trap, if you can.
Soundcloud wormhole nasty trap.
Music to rage to.)

*(*MARGOT *looms over* LOLA*,*
arms folded across her chest, watching.)

(And we watch LOLA *bike.*
At first, on a flat road, legs fast, low gear.
It's like flying.)

*(*ROWAN *looms over* LOLA*.*
arms folded across their chest, watching.)

*(*MARGOT *and* ROWAN *watch*
Shifting and moving to get a different angle,
Investigating LOLA*'s posture.*

LOLA *doesn't acknowledge them, but she shifts her form to their gaze.*
ROWAN *looks at* LOLA*'s shoulder,* LOLA *rolls it back and down.*
MARGOT *looks at* LOLA*'s hands,* LOLA *wiggles her fingers, loosens her grip.)*

*(*LOLA *shifts the gear of her bike*
She comes out of the saddle.
It's a climb.
Heavy, sticky, wheels in mud climb.
The investigation continues,
But LOLA *doesn't shift this time.*
Steady, solitary, grind through the climb.
Truth be told, it's a very ugly, sweaty climb.
It becomes fun.)

*(*LOLA *climbs.*
LOLA *doesn't shift anything this time.*
Heaving air in and out of her lungs.)

*(*AVERY *climbs down from his landing.)*

(We shift.)

THIRTEEN

*(*LOLA *and* AVERY*.*
They are sweaty and out of breath.
They collapse on the ground of the overlook.
Waters in hand.)

LOLA:
Fuck.

AVERY:
Right?

LOLA:
Fuck, that's *hard.*

AVERY:
It's the best climb.
The very best climb.

LOLA:
Fuck that climb.
My lungs

AVERY:
They're on fire, right?

(LOLA takes a deep sip.)

LOLA:
Goddamn.
Are you trying to kill me?

AVERY:
You liked it.

LOLA:
I did.
It hurts but like
So good.
It's like I'm not fighting my lungs.

AVERY:
No, you and your lungs are fighting the altitude.
You're a team.

LOLA:
They haven't burned like this since my first week here.

AVERY:
It sneaks up on you sometimes.
The whole eight thousand feet above sea level thing.

LOLA:
I know.
I'm so fucking tired.
All the time.

AVERY:
On that nine-hours-of-sleep-grind?

LOLA:
Nine's not enough.
I need like a full twenty-four.

AVERY:
And then probably like twenty-four hours to eat.

LOLA:
Completely.
Oh my god.
I'm ravenous.
All the time.

AVERY:
And you've gotta time that shit out.
Like I can't go do speed work if I've just housed three hamburgers.
But if you put a plate of hamburgers in front of me
Any time, any day
I'm gonna house it.

(LOLA *hesitates.)*

AVERY:
What?

LOLA:
Nope.

AVERY:
Say it.

LOLA:
It doesn't go away?

AVERY:
Being ravenous?

LOLA:
Insatiable.

AVERY:
No. It does not.

LOLA:
I just want
more of
Everything.

AVERY:
Absolutely everything.

LOLA:
How do you stop yourself from getting too fixated on it all?

AVERY:
I don't.
I can't.
If you figure it out, can you let me know?

LOLA:
I'm trying to keep an appreciation for it all, without…

AVERY:
Getting too hung up on every tiny ache
Or tipping too far into superficial thoughts?

LOLA:
Both, but I meant the latter.

AVERY:
I like that about you, you aren't chasing down aesthetics.

LOLA:
No, you know, I'm really not.

AVERY:
There's not a day I do this that I'm not
Specifically grateful for my heart
For my lungs
That my achilles tendon hasn't snapped
Things like that.
…
What?

LOLA:
You're so
Sincere?

AVERY:
I'm sincere all the time.
Thanks for finally noticing.
You're the one with the walls up.

(LOLA laughs.)

LOLA:
Fuck you, then stop trying to climb them.

AVERY:
We just climbed this entire mountainside on two wheels.

LOLA:
So you're climbing for the sake of climbing.
I'm just an exercise to you?

AVERY:
Are you gonna make me say it?

LOLA:
I've never made you do anything.

AVERY:
I'm climbing because
If you can believe it,
I like you
And you think I'm a person who is hot
In theory and in practice/
Which makes me think you like me, too.

LOLA:
I want to crawl into a hole right now.

AVERY:
No! Don't crawl, don't crawl.
It was flattering, it made my whole week.
It was a nice glimpse behind the walls.

LOLA:
Alright, so what else have you noticed from climbing over the walls.

AVERY:
Oh, I'm not over all them yet.

LOLA:
Yet?

AVERY:
I think there's something here
In this space between us
And something is stopping you
That's what I've noticed on the climb.
I'll keep climbing, though.
I love climbing.
It's my new favorite climb.

LOLA:
I'm
Trying to find a flaw in what you just said

AVERY:
Stop trying to just find a flaw.
I've got plenty of unhidden flaws.

LOLA:
I can't find one.

AVERY:
I'll give you one:
My confidence is a cover up.

LOLA:
Don't lie!

AVERY:
I'm not lying.

LOLA:
As flaws go, it's a pretty good one.

AVERY:
I'm trying to move slower.
Put a solid foundation under everything.

LOLA:
Is it working?

AVERY:
You tell me.

LOLA:
I haven't run yet.

AVERY:
But you are still holding back.

LOLA:
I promise you I am not.

AVERY:
So you don't zoom ahead of me on the bike so you can lock yourself back up into your head?

LOLA:
No, not consciously!

AVERY:
You don't jump right to your head when you start to feel things, even pride.

LOLA:
I
do
do that sometimes.
But that's not about you.

AVERY:
I think you let yourself look at me just long enough to start to feel something spark, and then you look away.
I think right now, you're avoiding my gaze because you realize
I've been paying attention and it makes you feel some kinda way.

LOLA:
So how do you think I should stop holding myself back.

AVERY:
I think you should kiss me.
Or I think you should let me kiss you.
If there's a difference to you.
Either is fine with me.

LOLA:
I do like you.

AVERY:
I know.
In theory, you do.

LOLA:
In practice!

AVERY:
In practice?

*(*AVERY *pulls* LOLA *in, close.
They linger there.)*

LOLA:
I spend time with you!
I like spending time with you.

AVERY:
Okay.

LOLA:
I don't spend time with anyone else!
I mean, Rowan, but I pay them.

AVERY:
We can maybe leave Rowan out of this conversation.

LOLA:
Okay.

AVERY:
Okay.

*(*LOLA *and* AVERY *kiss.*
They let each other.
After, a moment, MARGOT *from the landing, into the megaphone.)*

MARGOT:
Lola!

*(*AVERY *remains unaware.*
He climbs up to his landing.)

MARGOT:
Lola! What is your damage?
(She comes down from her landing.)

FOURTEEN

LOLA:
Margot, please don't.
Please, it was going really well.

(Into the megaphone:)

MARGOT:
LOLA, come BACK TO LUNCH.

LOLA:
Not the deepest cut, Margot,
I am begging you.

(Into the megaphone:)

MARGOT:
Lola, please just come back into the restaurant and order a drink.

LOLA:
Please, the sun was perfect
And there were birds singing
And he smelled like sweat and pepper
And his mouth was really soft,
Please let me have this.

(LOLA *tries putting her helmet on to bike away.*
MARGOT *comes all the way over to* LOLA.
MARGOT, *into the megaphone.* LOLA, *shooting to match volume.)*

MARGOT:
Lola, what's your damage?

LOLA:
My *damage?*

MARGOT:
Okay, not *damage.*

*(*MARGOT *stands in front of the bike and puts her hands on the handlebars.)*

LOLA:
Don't block me in.

MARGOT:
Don't leave without telling me what's wrong.

LOLA:
She's just so loud all the time.

MARGOT:
Anna?

LOLA:
Yes Anna.

MARGOT:
She cares about you.

LOLA:
Loudly.

MARGOT:
Honestly, how dare she.

LOLA:
Don't be sarcastic right now.

MARGOT:
I just want you to take a breath and come back to lunch.

LOLA:
Absolutely not.
I'm going.

MARGOT:
You don't have to ruin lunch

LOLA:
Ruin/lunch?
I didn't ruin lunch

MARGOT:
You haven't seen our friends in like, months.

LOLA:
Honestly, maybe that's okay

MARGOT:
They're our friends, Lola.

LOLA:
They're your friends.

MARGOT:
They love you.

LOLA:
They've got a funny way of showing it.

MARGOT:
By supporting you?

LOLA:
She yelled it, Margot.
She like, screamed at me when I came in and then
Everyone turned to look at me.

MARGOT:
If anyone turned, it was to stare at Anna for yelling.

LOLA:
It wasn't.
You don't get it.
I just know.

MARGOT:
Anna has body shit too,
You don't have a monopoly on that.

LOLA:
Anna stopped her work before she was finished, then.
And she should stop putting that shit onto me.

MARGOT:
Babe, I think there's a lot going on in your brain right now.

LOLA:
I'm saying, Margot, that as the person this is happening to
I get final say on what happened.

MARGOT:
We're trying to support you!

LOLA:
You aren't hearing what I'm saying.
They are not acting like my friends.

MARGOT:
Lo, no one knows how to be your friend right now!
You're making it impossible!

LOLA:
And you never stopped to ask yourself why I might be like this?

MARGOT:
Don't make this my fault.

LOLA:
You are fucking impossible, Margot.
You're sticking up for your friends

And honestly they're nightmares.
You're all an absolute nightmare.

(A moment)

LOLA:
I'm going to go.

MARGOT:
I'm going to have lunch.
Cool off.

LOLA:
No, like I'm really going to go.

MARGOT:
Whatever.
(She steps out of the way.)

*(*LOLA *gets on the bike.*
She bikes away, but Margot doesn't get any further away.
MARGOT *simply watches.*
LOLA *tries to pedal faster, but* MARGOT *still remains by her side.*
LOLA *unclips.*
She takes off her helmet.)

LOLA:
Am I going to relive it all forever?

*(*MARGOT *shrugs.)*

LOLA:
Are you going to be in my head forever?

*(*MARGOT *lowers the megaphone.)*

MARGOT:
Maybe.

*(*LOLA *watches as* MARGOT *ascends back to her perch.*
MARGOT *lowers her sunglasses over her eyes.*
We shift.)

FIFTEEN

(The transition from bike to run.
The click-click of unclipping from a bike.
A long, long drink of water.)

LOLA:
There are things they will not tell you—
The people who do not run
but tell you that maybe *you* should.
They will say things like
Just lace up a pair of shoes and go.
Just decide to do it.
It's so easy.
What they don't tell you
And what they might not even know, is
The shoes are expensive, maybe prohibitively so.
And to get the right shoes you should know how you run.
You have to get to know how you have moved your whole life until now.
That someone will have to tape your stride and play it back slow.
so you can watch what part of your foot hits the ground when you land.
Does your ankle roll inward?
or outward?
Will you be able to tell when you change?
When you're stronger?
When you have to pivot?
Or when you're injured
And you have to take a step back?
Are you committed to paying that much attention to yourself?
Can you handle thinking about your body that much?
(She throws her running shoes down onto the ground.)
What good has all the running done?
You can't really run away

It all just fucking follows you anyways.
All the things you thought you could leave behind,
All the things that build and build and build because you didn't tend to them when they were small
I don't know how much pressure my body can take anymore.
After all of this time,
Paying attention to every breath and move
I thought I would know myself well enough
To know if I could keep going.
But am I actually unable to do this?
Am I just setting myself up for a pass-fail evaluation of my own creating?
Do I even know why I'm doing this anymore?
I don't want to do it.
Most of this race is done,
And there are people waiting to slap sunscreen on me
And I am sitting on the ground next to my bike
And I don't want to do it.
(She pulls on the second shoe.)
(She stands.
We shift.)

RUN

SIXTEEN

*(*ROWAN *and* LOLA *approach.*
AVERY *waits at the lookout.)*

AVERY:
Oh!
You invited Rowan!

ROWAN:
You sound disappointed.

*(*AVERY *did.*
Sound disappointed)

AVERY:
Not at all!

ROWAN:
Two-thirds of the way through training, friends!
I heard there was pizza and beer!

AVERY:
Pizza in the box
Beer in the backpack

*(*AVERY *goes in to hug* ROWAN.
They duck out from under him.)

AVERY:
You feeling okay?

ROWAN:
Feeling like I haven't seen you in class lately.

AVERY:
The shop's been busy.

*(*ROWAN *opens the pizza box.*
They take a deep inhale.)

ROWAN:
Ugh, I can always fuck up this pizza.

AVERY:
You and every other person in Denver, it seems.
That's why I can't come to class.

ROWAN:
Excuses, babe.

AVERY:
Whatever, you're missing out on the hugs.

ROWAN:
Come to class, I'll hug you there.
(They take a giant bite of pizza.
They make a show of it.)

AVERY:
Come to the shop, I'll hug you there.

ROWAN:
I don't need hugs.

LOLA:
Everyone need hugs.

ROWAN:
Not / today.

AVERY:
I like / hugs.

LOLA:
Everyone needs hugs.
Four hugs a day for survival.
Eight for maintenance.
You have to want them, like it doesn't count if you don't want it
Because you're too busy being in a heightened /state

AVERY:
Do you want a hug?

LOLA:
What?

AVERY:
You only know like two people in this city.
By that logic we should both hug you twice a day.

ROWAN:
(To LOLA*)* When you are no longer my client, we can hug.
You gotta get all your hugs from him, sorry!

AVERY:
If you want them, right?

LOLA:
I would hug you.

AVERY:
How do we do it for maximum scientific benefit?

*(*MARGOT *pulls out a pair of binoculars to watch.*
ROWAN *laughs.)*

ROWAN:
Avery, get the fuck out.
I think you know what makes a good hug.

*(*AVERY *and* LOLA *hug.*
Acknowledge the fact that getting into a hug with someone for the first time is awkward.
And then, it's rather nice.
After a moment, ROWAN *cracks a beer to break the moment.)*

ROWAN:
That was intimate.
Have you been reading up on human contact while you've been here avoiding most human contact?

LOLA:
My ex specialized in it.
Like, literally.
She does research on human contact.

ROWAN:
Is that why she keeps trying to virtually contact you?

LOLA:
Irrelevant.

ROWAN:
Sustained.

LOLA:
Most of her work is with babies.

AVERY:
So you dated a saint?

LOLA:
I wouldn't go as far as saint.

AVERY:
Sounds like—

ROWAN:
Pizza?

(They hold out the box to LOLA.
LOLA *takes it and takes a slice.*
She doesn't take a bite.)

ROWAN:
So how is your training, Avery,
I'd have no way of knowing / considering you don't show up to class—

AVERY:
I didn't hire you this year.

ROWAN:
I still get to ask.

AVERY:
You aren't asking, you're guilting.

ROWAN:
Will you get to the finish line this year?

AVERY:
Unnecessary.

LOLA:
Did you quit a race?

AVERY:
Yeah, I just wasn't in it.

ROWAN:
It should be noted that was the first year he didn't train with me.
The only year you DNF.
I'm just saying maybe there's a trend there.

AVERY:
I'm the one that sent Lola to you.
You're good, we know.

ROWAN:
I just like to hear it.

AVERY:
Lola,
You can DNF if you need to.

LOLA:
I don't want to DNF.
Do you think I'm going / to DNF

ROWAN:
You won't fucking DNF.
Do you think she's going to DNF?

AVERY:
There is no shame in not finishing.

ROWAN:
She'll finish.

AVERY:
Okay!
Okay.

LOLA:
…
Now I'm worried.

ROWAN:
Fix your mess.

AVERY:
Lola, you'll be fine.
You want it more than you don't want it.
Just remember your reason for being here.

LOLA:
What?

ROWAN:
I didn't / say—

AVERY:
I'm just saying we all have a thing.
We're all old enough to not do the things we don't want to do
and if we're here, and we are paying a lot of money to do this thing,
there has to be something that brought us here.
Or keeps us here at least.
And some people's reasons might feel bigger than others to you,
but they all feel momentous to the people competing.
That's why we do it.

LOLA:
Oh.

AVERY:
That's why race morning feels so wild.
It's everyone's drive and passion buzzing in their veins.
And if you stop feeling that passion, then you stop racing.

ROWAN:
Mmm.

AVERY:
Or,
You know,
you race until you can't anymore.
You can't plan for accidents obviously.

*(AVERY waits for ROWAN to say something.
They don't.)*

AVERY:
Just channel your brain to the moments right before you let them charge you hundreds of dollars.
Everyone's like my dad died.
Or I'm going through a crisis of faith.
Or I lost a fuck ton of weight.

LOLA:
Did you?

AVERY:
Lose a fuck ton of weight?
No.
I don't mean these are my specifics, I just mean everyone's got a specific.

ROWAN:
You're just addicted to endorphins, Avery.

AVERY:
You've got everything you need to finish the race already.
I didn't mean to scare you.

*(AVERY waits for LOLA to say something.
She doesn't.)*

AVERY:
I feel like I said something wrong.

LOLA:
You didn't.

AVERY:
You both got really quiet.

ROWAN:
Don't pick at it, Ave.
Have some pizza.

AVERY:
I'm not picking,
I thought I was helping

ROWAN:
Okay.

AVERY:
…
I'm gonna go.

ROWAN:
That's not what I meant.

AVERY:
You can finish the beers.
Please.
(He picks up a helmet.)

LOLA:
Don't go.

AVERY:
Nah,
I know when to quit when I'm too far behind,
Especially when no one wants to catch me up.
It's clear you don't want this.
For whatever reason, you didn't want to hang with just me
So / you just brought them
Instead of just telling me

LOLA:
That's not / it.

ROWAN:
I invited myself.

AVERY:
And you're covering for her with every breath, so
I'm just going to go.
For what it's worth, Lola,
I don't think you're going to DNF.
You're so singularly focused on this
Clearly it's all you want,
And you want it a lot,
And I think that's the only thing you need to get you through it.
(He puts on his helmet.
We shift.)

SEVENTEEN

(LOLA, *running.*
MARGOT *has descended close to the ground.)*

MARGOT:
You gonna tell him?

LOLA:
No.

MARGOT:
You think Rowan's gonna tell him?

LOLA:
No.

MARGOT:
Are you feeling paranoid?

LOLA:
No.

MARGOT:
You think he's gonna find out.

LOLA:
No.

MARGOT:
I think he's gonna find out.

LOLA:
No.

MARGOT:
You hugged him.
Before it got fucked.

LOLA:
Yes.

MARGOT:
Did you soak in that moment?
Did it smell like sweat and pepper?

LOLA:
Please, do not…

MARGOT:
You've been stressing your muscles a lot lately,
You know what's stronger than morphine?
The lil chemicals that come from a hug.

LOLA:
A hug that you want.

MARGOT:
You wanted it.
You want to do it again?
You'll have to explain yourself if you want to do it again.

LOLA:
I don't know.

MARGOT:
Four, eight, twelve—you haven't forgotten.

LOLA:
Nope.

MARGOT:
Are you getting four hugs a day for survival?

LOLA:
I have a gravity blanket.

MARGOT:
Are you getting eight hugs a day for maintenance?

LOLA:
Twenty-five pound gravity blanket.

MARGOT:
Are you going to let him hug you twelve times a day for growth?

LOLA:
You bought me the gravity blanket.

MARGOT:
You could also just go in for one big twenty second long hug.
I bet he'd go for it.
One big apology hug.

LOLA:
Margot.

MARGOT:
The gravity blanket is fine but even then,
The way we're all living these days,
No one's really getting enough contact
I mean, statistically / speaking—

LOLA:
You want statistics?
Fine.
Do you remember the first time we really hung out one on one.

MARGOT:
Washington Square Park.

LOLA:
We were right there with dripping ice cream.
You said
(She reaches up and takes the megaphone from MARGOT.*)*
(She holds the megaphone up to her mouth.)
My job is mostly statistics, it's less glamorous than you think.
(Megaphone down)
And I said
(Megaphone up)
Give yourself some credit.
Numbers can make beautiful things.
Washington Square Park is one mile in circumference.
Exactly.

MARGOT:
Perfect city planning.

LOLA:
So I bet somewhere in your statistics, there are beautiful, human things.

(Megaphone down)

LOLA:
And you said

*(*LOLA *holds the megaphone up to* MARGOT*'s mouth and waits.)*

MARGOT:
Even when couples are fighting
They should hug
Often.
That's what I know.

(Megaphone down)

LOLA:
You were the one who taught me there was something

beautiful about contact.
There was something really healing.
And we hugged.
For twenty seconds.
We counted together.

MARGOT:
Yes.

LOLA:
It had been four months, three weeks, and three days.
Since I'd last had a hug.
And I've only been in Colorado for four months.

MARGOT:
Oh.

LOLA:
You stopped hugging me.

MARGOT:
Oh.

LOLA:
For weeks.

MARGOT:
Oh.

LOLA:
All I did was notice it.

(We shift.)

EIGHTEEN

*(*LOLA *runs.*
Alone
We watch her pick up speed.
ROWAN *catches up.)*

ROWAN:
Okay, I have been looking for you.

LOLA:
Just running around town?

ROWAN:
Since you ran through town and *got into some collision.*

LOLA:
How did you know that?
Do you have a drone following me?

ROWAN:
I put myself into your watch as an emergency contact.

LOLA:
What?
When?

ROWAN:
When I set up your statistic sharing.

*(*LOLA *looks at her watch.)*

LOLA:
That's a function on this thing??

ROWAN:
Well it seems like it was necessary
I just got an alert you got hit?
What was it?
A car?

LOLA:
It was minor.

ROWAN:
The impact was enough for your watch to register it as an incident.

LOLA:
I'm fine.

ROWAN:
"Oh, I'm fine, you should see the other guy" doesn't work when the other guy is a Subaru.

LOLA:
I got tapped.
Garmin is overreacting.

ROWAN:
Lola, you were supposed to do a short run today and then put your feet up.

LOLA:
I'll put them up still.

ROWAN:
Lola, stop running.

LOLA:
No.

ROWAN:
Lola, you can stop running.

LOLA:
I can't.

ROWAN:
Yes, you can.
That's the best and worst part about running.
If you don't want to be doing it anymore, you just stop.

LOLA:
No.
Because if I stop running, I start hurting.
And if I start hurting, I'm going to feel like I can never do it again.
Like I waited too late and my body has congealed into the shell of a person who waited too long and now is destined to sit, hunch-backed at a desk for the rest of eternity.

ROWAN:
Not true.

LOLA:
How do you know?

ROWAN:
Because I have a degree in this.
And several certifications.

LOLA:
But you aren't in this body.

ROWAN:
Okay, sometimes that's a valid answer, but trust me here—
You still have at *least* five years before your body is completely done fusing itself together.
You're still molding.
You still have time to mold.
But not if you overwork yourself.
Not if you overtrain.

*(*LOLA *slows down.*
It's closer to a jog or a speed walk.
She's still moving.)

ROWAN:
Why did you hire me if you weren't going to listen to me?
Because this right here?
This is the bullshit.

LOLA:
No, it's this or nothing.
Literally nothing.
I don't have an apartment to go back to.
I don't have a life to pick back up.
I just have this.
So I'm doing it.

ROWAN:
Do you want your apartment back?

LOLA:
No!

ROWAN:
Do you want your life back?

LOLA:
I want a life back.

ROWAN:
That's different.
Stop running.
Or jogging.

(LOLA begins to bullshit bounce.
It's slow, but she's going through the motions of running completely.
Looks a bit like moonwalking.
Bullshit bounce)

LOLA:
This is what you get.

ROWAN:
I can't take you seriously when you do this.

LOLA:
Good, you'll stop telling me to stop.

ROWAN:
I need you to understand that sometimes discipline is knowing when to stop.
You're going to burn out.
You have to think of the big picture.

LOLA:
Everything, Rowan
Everything is new.
Every day is a series of new decisions.

ROWAN:
Do you know why I stopped racing?

LOLA:
No, I have not scaled that brick wall of your personal life yet and you know it.

(Bullshit bounce)

ROWAN:
I am literally broken.
I am forbidden from distance running by my PT.
One would argue that what I'm doing right now is not smart, trying to keep up with you.

LOLA:
This is why I'm doing the bull shit bounce for you.

ROWAN:
I have two knee replacements.
A series of healed but tedious stress fractures up my right leg.
Leading to constantly stressed calves.
The activation I have to do before I take off is absurd.
And then in the last marathon I completed, I twisted my ankle at mile 9
A second grade ankle tear.
It was so bad that when Avery twisted his ankle
All he could do was worry it was as bad as mine
And he couldn't get out of his head and he quit the damn race.
I slipped on someone else's discarded energy chew
Really fucking stupid
Really shit luck from the world
And I always think if I had been paying more attention, I would have avoided it
I *could* have, maybe, I guess I'll never know.
I'm not supposed to run anymore.
Not the way I used to, at least.
And running is my life.
And I've been trying everything to get that high back.
Including swimming, which I detest.

LOLA:
That day at the lake.

ROWAN:
Haunts me.
I play it back all the time.
I wish I'd said anything else.

*(*LOLA *stops bull shit bouncing.*
They walk.)

ROWAN:
And then you showed up in class.
I knew who you were from the start and the fact you didn't leave class
That was
That was strength.
And you kept coming back and I was like god
She is either fucking fearless or scared to death or both
And I get that.
I feel a particular kinship to that.
But I'm still trying to figure out how to be strong like that.
You are one of the strongest people I know.
I mean that.
Intimidatingly so, sometimes.
Because you keep showing up for yourself and most people don't do that.
But my strength?
This endurance?
This will fade.
I'll replace it with a different kind of strength, of course,
But the body I live in right now as a runner will change when I'm not running
Maybe not drastically
But it will be different.
I will not be able to do the things I used to do.
The things I thought made me the person I am.
I am having a hard time with that in a way that isn't flattering.

I am face-to-face with my own nasty ableist tendencies right now
And you came in with a root in what you can do
And I am losing what I love to do
But I'm not losing all the things I can do.
I just have to stop for a moment
And evaluate what I can do
What my body will let me do.
I need to rest, Lola.
You need to rest.
Because worth
Worth isn't in what you look like
Or what your body can do.

LOLA:
Well, where is it then?
Where is the worth?

ROWAN:
It just is.
It's just there.
The worth.
Your worth is just there.
...
I'm living vicariously through you
I want you to get your glory.
You've worked really hard for it.
You deserve your glory.

LOLA:
I feel like I'm running into the ground and I can't stop.

ROWAN:
What are you running away from?
What are you worried is going to catch up to you?

LOLA:
God, everything.

(A moment)

ROWAN:
Confront it first.

(We shift.)

NINETEEN

*(*LOLA *climbs the vertical space, not very high, but enough for a new perspective.*
MARGOT, *for real this time.*
Headphones over or in her ears.
Holding her phone in one hand and maybe a coffee cup in her hand.
New York buzzes around her.)

MARGOT:
Oh my god, did you call me on purpose?

LOLA:
Did you not want to talk?
You've been calling so much I thought you wanted to talk
I can hang up?

MARGOT:
No, no, my god don't hang up
I was just surprised.

LOLA:
I think I finally have the words.

MARGOT:
Are you running?

LOLA:
No, I'm hiking.
I'm just a little out of breath

MARGOT:
Why?

LOLA:
The air is thin?

MARGOT:
No, why are you…hiking?

LOLA:
Because it's Sunday and usually on Sundays I long run
But I am trying to take it easier.

MARGOT:
Can you like,
Explain all of that to me from the beginning?

LOLA:
No.
Look.
I've got someone to sublease my apartment
So stop going around, okay?

MARGOT:
Are you ever coming back?

LOLA:
I need you to stop coming around.
I need you to stop calling.
I need you to stop reaching out.

MARGOT:
I think we should talk, though.
Now that you've had space.
Mountains of space, apparently.

LOLA:
You don't want to be near me.

MARGOT:
That's so obviously not true.

LOLA:
No, M, you didn't want to be near me when I was in Manhattan either.

MARGOT:
I didn't know how to be near you for a while there.
You were so closed off, you were—

LOLA:
Did you ask?

MARGOT:
Would that have gone over well?

LOLA:
Did. You. Ask.

MARGOT:
No.

LOLA:
When we first started…

MARGOT:
Dating?

LOLA:
It wasn't dating at first.
You were adamant about that.
You didn't want to.

MARGOT:
I didn't have the time.

LOLA:
You would have made the time if you wanted to.
In fact, you eventually made the time.

MARGOT:
I grew into us, yes.

LOLA:
No, I shrank into someone you'd make time for.

MARGOT:
Absolutely untrue.

LOLA:
I'm asking you to entertain the idea that I might be

right
And
That you weren't consciously aware of it.

(Silence
Well, breathing)

LOLA:
Your friends

MARGOT:
Our friends

LOLA:
Your friends know very little about me
And they ask about my workouts
And they remark on my meal choices
And they assume I'm ordering vodka waters
It doesn't seem malicious to you.

MARGOT:
What should we have been talking to you about, then?

LOLA:
Anything.
What did we talk about before?
Science. Hugs. Politics.
Good books.
Assholes at work.
Coffee preferences and
Where we want to travel and
We would talk about Paris
And Brussels
And The Netherlands
And about not understanding ballet
And our mothers.
But you wouldn't let me near your friends before
For a really long time, it felt like you didn't want to be seen with me.
I'm not saying that's the whole truth, but that's what it felt like.

And then after,
I wasn't a person
I was a shrunken and further shrinking body.
And I tried to be a person and we would always default back to me being a shell.
And part of that is on me,
I feel like I started to hide myself away from you
So much that I was hiding myself from myself too.
I got so lost that I had to
Actually get lost to find myself again.
I think I actually like who I am?
And I don't want to be a person who runs away when things get hard.
I want to be a person who shows up for myself.
I want to be me,
I want the people around me to know who I am.
And if they don't like who I really am,
I can find people who do.
So
Sorry, I guess,
For not letting you see me.

MARGOT:
. . .
This is really hard to hear.

LOLA:
This is really hard to say.

MARGOT:
I'm sorry.

LOLA:
It's okay,
just please stop calling me.

MARGOT:
Okay.

LOLA:
God, I've been so scared to have this conversation.

(A moment)

MARGOT:
Can I ask you one more thing?

LOLA:
You can ask.
I might not answer.

MARGOT:
Why Colorado?

LOLA:
The Boulder Half Iron.

MARGOT:
Like a giant triathlon?

LOLA:
70.3 miles.

MARGOT:
God, I bet that final .3 is so annoying.

LOLA:
It does feel added on just to fuck with me.

MARGOT:
Are you letting people help you?

LOLA:
Trying to.
Like pulling teeth.

MARGOT:
Can I wish you luck?
Or is that bad luck?

(Likely a smile)

LOLA:
I have no idea.

MARGOT:
Like how all dancers say shit to one another / before a performance?

LOLA:
Yeah, truly no clue.

MARGOT:
Well. Shit, Lola.

LOLA:
Shit, Margot.

*(*LOLA *and* MARGOT *hang up.*
MARGOT *leaves.*
LOLA *descends.)*

TWENTY

*(*LOLA, AVERY
The overlook.
He runs up.
They look at each other for a second.)

AVERY:
You wrote me a novel in a text message.

LOLA:
I had a lot to say.
I was leaving a lot out, it wasn't fair to you.

AVERY:
You could have told me all along.
I don't say that to make you feel guilty,
I just …
I always want the whole truth.

LOLA:
I was really scared, Avery.
I am really scared.

AVERY:
Are you scared right now?

*(*LOLA *nods.)*

AVERY:
Do you want a hug?

LOLA:
Do you?

AVERY:
Yeah.

(Inhale
LOLA *and* AVERY *hug.)*

LOLA:
Oh, hugs.

AVERY:
Oh, damn.
Yeah.

(Exhale)

AVERY:
I like you because you let me see you fall in love with moving.
I got a front row seat to you realizing this is a way you love to move.
And I love to move like this, too.
It felt like our whys at the end of the day were the exact same.
Does that help explain it?

LOLA:
Why didn't you just say that?

AVERY:
I didn't want to come on too strong.
You showed up and I wanted to hit the gas.
And I was just worried it was all too much.
So I got stuck.
And I am really bad when I feel stuck.

LOLA:
I get that.

AVERY:
Training for this thing makes me feel in motion.
Training alongside you.
For me it about the time spent.

LOLA:
Oh.
It really isn't about what I look like to you.

AVERY:
No.
I mean.
Fuck.
I do—I am—I

LOLA:
I get it.
It's not what it's about to me.
But I do.

AVERY:
Find me attractive?

LOLA:
Yeah.

AVERY:
Oh, thank god.

LOLA:
Was that up for debate?

AVERY:
Sometimes I have to hear it!

LOLA:
Oh, Avery, it's about / the time spent.

AVERY:
The time spent. /
Shit.

LOLA:
Does this qualify as letting all the pieces fall and seeing where they land?

(AVERY *laughs.)*

AVERY:
No, you don't even know the half of it yet.
Every race is different, but there's such a different view from the other side.
There's a moment before you attempt something like this and there's a moment after.
It's hard to explain.

LOLA:
Perspective.

AVERY:
Mhmm.

LOLA:
Learning by doing.

AVERY:
Yes.

LOLA:
How do you know the race won't make me worse.

AVERY:
I don't.
But I'm willing to find out.

LOLA:
Oh.

AVERY:
Tell me all of it after?
We're going to be so tired we won't want to move.
You can sit in my compression boots and we can drink beer and we can
Find out

All the things
Slowly.

LOLA:
That sounds really nice.

(A moment)

AVERY:
You know, they say the training is the hard part.
The race is just a celebration.
It's a dance.

LOLA:
Swim. Bike. Run. Dance.

AVERY:
You look ready to dance with the Rockies, Lola.

LOLA:
Do the mountains dance?

AVERY:
You say that like you haven't been dancing with the Rockies for as long as you've been here.

LOLA:
Is that what that was, when I first landed?
That feeling?

AVERY:
Mama Nature sweeping you right off your feet.

LOLA:
Mountain Man.

AVERY:
Manhattan Proper.

LOLA:
You're right.
I am ready to dance.

*(A moment.
We shift.)*

THE FINISH LINE

LOLA:
There is a point where it is miserable.
Really fucking miserable.
The sweat has dried into salt and we have been moving for so long.
No music in our ears for distraction.
No crowd around to cheer us on.
We're just trudging forward.
And yeah forward is forward no matter how slow
And yes the elites go fast and it's over
And that's amazing
But there's something more amazing about
Being on your feet for so long.
The back of the pack can do things the front of the pack wouldn't dream of
They can keep going
And to keep going right now
In this moment
I can put it all down,
The things people believed of me
Or said about me
All of the weight of my own expectations
The things I said about myself
Whether they were right or wrong
Forgive myself for holding myself back
Forgive myself for the years where I could have been more free

It just doesn't matter!
I can be free *now,*
And I realize that these miles
They're nothing but the beginning of a very large climb up to who I could be
Who I already am.
Who I was the whole time.
I can finally see it.
Literally.
I can see the finish line stretched out in front of me.
I see the archway
I see the time mat on the ground
I see the distance my feet will cover shrinking
I feel my heart speed up and time stretches like saltwater taffy
Pulling at my muscles
Bearing my guts
Each millisecond its own memory of how I got here.
And it feels like nothing I've ever felt before.
Like the things inside of me have expanded so much,
I can no longer contain it
I am so full that I could burst
I feel like I have reached the peak of all that life has to offer
Feel this absolute rush,
Feel my body expand and stretch out to its limit
And then, in a moment,
I feel really small.
And I remember when I got to Colorado,
Standing in front of the Rockies and I understand
I feel small
But ready to explode
And so I do.
(She picks up the pace for the finish.)

END OF PLAY

www.ingramcontent.com/pod-product-compliance
Ingram Content Group UK Ltd.
Pitfield, Milton Keynes, MK11 3LW, UK
UKHW022006190726
13853UKWH00004B/1762

9 798888 560457